WORKBOOK FOR SEEING BEAUTIFUL AGAIN

50 Devotions to Find Redemption in Every Part of Your Story – Practical Guide to Lysa TerKeurst's Book

Barnes Publishers

This Workbook is a companion tool to be used alongside the original book. It is not a replacement for the original book, nor does it contain the full text of the original book. It is intended to be a supplemental resource to help readers reflect on the key lessons and takeaways from the original book.

TABLE OF CONTENTS

How to Use This Workbook 9

Introduction 13

    The Original Book Summary 13

The Process Before the Promise........................... 17

    Journaling Prompts:....................................... 17

    Key Lessons: 17

    Self-Reflection Questions: 19

The Best Place to Park Your Mind Today............... 23

    Journaling Prompts:...................................... 23

    Key Lessons: 23

    Self-Reflection Questions: 25

I Don't Want This to Be a Part of My Story........... 29

    Journaling Prompts:...................................... 29

    Key Lessons: 29

    Self-Reflection Questions: 31

Is This News or Truth?....................................... 35

Journaling Prompts:................................35

Key Lessons: 35

Self-Reflection Questions: 37

When Joy Feels So Very Unrealistic 41

Journaling Prompts:................................ 41

Key Lessons: 41

Self-Reflection Questions: 43

When Joy Feels So Very Unrealistic 47

Journaling Prompts:................................ 47

Key Lessons: 47

Self-Reflection Questions: 49

Why Would You Let This Happen, God? 53

Journaling Prompts:................................53

Key Lessons: 54

Self-Reflection Questions: 55

Step After Step of Unwavering Obedience............59

Journaling Prompts:................................59

Key Lessons: 60

Self-Reflection Questions: 62

Three Questions to Ask Before Giving a Response You Can't Take Back.................................. 67

Journaling Prompts:.. 67

Key Lessons: 68

Self-Reflection Questions: 70

Is It Really That Big of a Deal If I Stay Offended? . 75

Journaling Prompts:.. 75

Key Lessons: 76

Self-Reflection Questions: 77

This Won't Be For Nothing 81

Journaling Prompts:.. 81

Key Lessons: 81

Self-Reflection Questions: 83

The Only Love That Never Fails............................87

Journaling Prompts:..87

Key Lessons: 87

Self-Reflection Questions: 89

When I Deny Jesus 93

   Journaling Prompts: 93

   Key Lessons: 94

   Self-Reflection Questions: 95

Three Perspectives to Remember When Your Normal Gets Hijacked 99

   Journaling Prompts: 99

   Key Lessons: 100

   Self-Reflection Questions: 101

Saved by Suffering 105

   Journaling Prompts: 105

   Key Lessons: 106

   Self-Reflection Questions: 107

Sometimes It's a One- or Two-Verse Day 111

   Journaling Prompts: 111

   Key Lessons: 112

   Self-Reflection Questions: 113

When Things Get Worse Just Before They Get Better 117

Journaling Prompts:.....................................117

Key Lessons: 117

Self-Reflection Questions: 119

The Blessings of Boundaries 123

Journaling Prompts:..................................... 123

Key Lessons: 123

Self-Reflection Questions: 125

Where Is My Happily Ever After? 129

Journaling Prompts:..................................... 129

Key Lessons: 129

Self-Reflection Questions: 131

When Giving Grace Feels Hard........................... 135

Journaling Prompts:..................................... 135

Key Lessons: 135

Self-Reflection Questions: 137

Forgiveness: The Double-Edged Word 141

Journaling Prompts:.....................................141

Key Lessons: 141

Self-Reflection Questions: 143

Self-Evaluation Questions..................................... 147

How to Use This Workbook

Welcome to the companion workbook for Seeing Beautiful Again: 50 Devotions to Find Redemption in Every Part of Your Story by Lysa TerKeurst. This Workbook is designed to enhance your understanding of the original book and help you apply its key concepts and lessons meaningfully to your own life. To make the most of this Workbook, follow the guidelines below:

Start with the Summary: Begin by reading the summary of the original book provided at the beginning of this Workbook. This summary serves as a quick refresher of the main points and ideas discussed in the book. It will help you recall the core concepts before delving deeper into each chapter.

Journaling Prompts: After reading the summary, each chapter includes journaling prompts. These prompts are intended to encourage introspection and self-discovery. Take your time to reflect on the questions and jot down your thoughts, feelings, and insights in the space provided. Journaling can be a powerful tool for personal growth and a better understanding of the material.

Key Lessons: In each chapter, you will find key lessons derived from the corresponding section in the original book. These lessons distill the core takeaways and principles. As you progress through the Workbook, consider how these lessons resonate with your experiences and beliefs. Reflect on how you can apply these lessons to various aspects of your life.

Self-Reflection Questions: Alongside the key lessons, there are self-reflection questions. These questions encourage critical thinking and a deeper exploration of the book's themes. Engage with these questions thoughtfully and honestly, as they will help you gain personal insights and a deeper connection with the material.

Self-Evaluation Section: Towards the end of the Workbook, you will encounter a section titled "Self-Evaluation Questions." This section aims to gauge your progress and growth throughout the Workbook. Please answer these questions sincerely, assessing how the exercises and reflections have impacted your understanding and perspective.

Go at Your Own Pace: This Workbook is meant to be a personal journey, so go at a comfortable pace. There's no rush; take as much time as you need to explore the material thoroughly and integrate the lessons into your life.

Use Your Original Book: It is highly recommended to have a copy of the original book with you while using this Workbook. Whenever a concept, quote, or idea sparks your interest, refer back to the relevant section in the original book for a more comprehensive understanding.

Share and Discuss: Feel free to share your insights and progress with others. Discussions with friends, family, or a study group can provide fresh perspectives and enrich your learning experience.

Remember, this Workbook is a tool for personal growth and understanding. Embrace the process and be open to discovering new insights about yourself and the world around you. Happy learning and self-discovery!

Introduction

The Original Book Summary

"Seeing Beautiful Again: 50 Devotions to Find Redemption in Every Part of Your Story" by Lysa TerKeurst is a powerful and inspiring book that offers hope and healing to those struggling with pain, loss, or disappointment. Through 50 heartfelt and insightful devotions, TerKeurst guides readers on finding beauty and redemption in every aspect of their lives.

TerKeurst draws from her own experiences of heartbreak and loss, providing a candid and relatable perspective that resonates with readers. She shares how she discovered that even amid pain and brokenness, beauty is waiting to be seen and embraced.

The book covers various topics, such as navigating through grief, finding strength in vulnerability, embracing new beginnings, and experiencing the transformative power of God's love and grace.

TerKeurst combines biblical wisdom with practical insights throughout the devotions, offering tangible guidance and encouragement for those seeking healing and restoration. She emphasizes the importance of embracing our stories, acknowledging the reality of pain and recognizing that God can redeem and bring beauty out of even the most difficult circumstances.

The book is written in a warm and compassionate tone, making it accessible and comforting for readers amid their struggles. TerKeurst shares vulnerable stories from her life and integrates them with relevant scriptures, prayers, and reflection questions, making it an ideal resource for personal study or group discussion.

"Seeing Beautiful Again" is a source of hope and encouragement, providing readers with the tools and insights to navigate through hardships and emerge with a renewed sense of Purpose and perspective. It reminds readers that their stories matter and that God is actively working to bring redemption and beauty into every part of their lives.

Overall, "Seeing Beautiful Again" is a powerful and transformative book that offers comfort, healing, and renewed hope to anyone seeking redemption in their own story. Lysa TerKeurst's heartfelt words and practical guidance make this book a valuable resource for those on their journey towards healing and restoration.

The Process Before the Promise

Journaling Prompts:

1. Reflect on a situation where you have felt stagnant or stuck in the waiting process. How can you shift your perspective to see the beauty and Purpose in the process before the promise?

2. Consider a promise or dream you are currently waiting to fulfil. Journal about the lessons you have learned and the personal growth you have experienced during this waiting period.

Key Lessons:

1. Embracing the Process: Reflect on embracing the process before the promise. Explore how patience, surrender, and trust play a role in our personal growth and aligning with God's timing.

2. Finding Purpose in the Waiting: Contemplate finding Purpose and meaning in the waiting season.

Reflect on the lessons, character development, and strength gained as we navigate the process before the promise.

3. Strengthening Faith: Explore how the waiting process can strengthen our faith. Reflect on how relying on God's promises and relying on His faithfulness can deepen our trust and reliance on Him.

Self-Reflection Questions:

1. How have you typically approached waiting periods in your life? How can you shift your perspective to see the beauty and Purpose in the process before the promise?

_____

_____

_____

_____

_____

_____

2. Reflect on a promise or dream you are currently waiting to fulfil. What lessons have you learned during this waiting period? How has it shaped your character or transformed your perspective?

_____

_____

_____

_____

_____

_____

3. Understand the importance of embracing the process before the promise. How can you practice patience, surrender, and trust during the waiting seasons? What practical steps can you take to align with God's timing?

_____

_____

_____

_____

_____

_____

_____

4. Contemplate finding Purpose and meaning in the waiting season. How can you actively seek and discover the lessons, character development, and

strength that can be gained during this process? How can you make the most of this waiting period?

_____

_____

_____

_____

_____

_____

_____

5. Reflect on how the waiting process can strengthen your faith. In what ways have you experienced God's faithfulness and provision during times of waiting? How can you deepen your trust and reliance on Him amid uncertainty and unanswered prayers?

_____

_____

_____

_____

The Best Place to Park Your Mind Today

Journaling Prompts:

1. Reflect on the challenges and distractions that often consume your thoughts and mind. How can you intentionally shift your focus and find the best place to park your mind today?

2. Consider a specific situation or circumstance causing anxiety or worry. Journal about how you can surrender that situation to God and choose to align your thoughts with His truth and promises.

Key Lessons:

1. Choosing Where to Park Your Mind: Reflect on the power of choice in directing our thoughts. Explore how intentionally choosing where to park our minds can impact our mindset, emotions, and overall well-being.

2. The Power of Positive Thinking: Contemplate the influence of positive thinking on our perspective and outlook on life. Reflect on how focusing on gratitude, hope, and God's promises can transform our thinking patterns.

3. Surrendering to God's Truth: Explore the significance of surrendering our worries, fears, and anxieties to God. Reflect on how anchoring our minds in His truth and promises can bring peace, strength, and a renewed sense of Purpose.

Self-Reflection Questions:

1. What challenges or distractions often consume your thoughts and mind? How can you intentionally shift your focus and find the best place to park your mind today?

_____

_____

_____

_____

_____

_____

2. Reflect on a specific situation or circumstance causing anxiety or worry. How can you surrender that situation to God and choose to align your thoughts with His truth and promises?

_____

_____

_____

_____

_____

_____

3. Understand the power of choice in directing your thoughts. How can you actively choose where to park your mind to impact your mindset, emotions, and overall well-being positively?

_____

_____

_____

_____

_____

_____

4. Contemplate the influence of positive thinking on your perspective and outlook on life. How can you cultivate gratitude, hope, and trust in God's promises? What practical ways to shift your thoughts to focus on the positive?

_____

_____

_____

_____

_____

_____

5. Reflect on surrendering your worries, fears, and anxieties to God. How can you actively anchor your mind in His truth and promises? What scriptures or affirmations can you cling to bring peace, strength, and a renewed sense of Purpose?

_____

_____

_____

_____

_____

_____

28

I Don't Want This to Be a Part of My Story

Journaling Prompts:

1. Reflect on a challenging or painful event in your life that you have struggled to accept as a part of your story. How can you shift your perspective and find beauty or redemption in that experience?

2. Consider the power of rewriting your narrative. Journal how you can reclaim and transform your story into one that empowers, inspires, and showcases your resilience.

Key Lessons:

1. Embracing Our Whole Story: Reflect on embracing all parts of our story, even the difficult and unwanted aspects. Explore how accepting these parts can lead to healing, growth, and finding beauty in unexpected places.

2. Redefining the Impact: Contemplate how to redefine the impact of challenging events in our lives. Reflect on how these experiences can shape our character, provide valuable lessons, and offer opportunities for personal transformation and strength.

3. Finding Redemption and Purpose: Explore the concept of finding redemption and Purpose in every part of our story. Reflect on how God can bring beauty out of pain and use our experiences to bring healing, hope, and inspiration to others.

Self-Reflection Questions:

1. Think about a challenging event or season in your life that you have struggled to accept. How can you shift your perspective and find beauty or redemption in that experience?

_____

_____

_____

_____

_____

_____

2. Reflect on embracing all parts of your story, even the difficult and unwanted aspects. How can you accept and acknowledge these parts of your story?

_____

_____

_____

_____

_____

_____

3. Contemplate how you can redefine the impact of challenging events in your life. How have these experiences shaped your character and provided valuable lessons? How can you use them as an opportunity for personal transformation and growth?

_____

_____

_____

_____

_____

_____

4. Explore finding redemption and Purpose in every part of your story. How can you believe that God can bring beauty out of pain? In what ways can your experiences bring healing, hope, and inspiration to others?

_____

_____

_____

_____

_____

_____

5. Reflect on how you can reclaim your story and transform it into one that empowers, inspires, and showcases your resilience. What steps can you take to rewrite your narrative and shift it towards a more positive and empowering direction?

_____

_____

_____

_____

_____

_____

34

Is This News or Truth?

Journaling Prompts:

1. Reflect on a recent news story or information that has affected you emotionally or mentally. How can you discern between news and truth to process and respond healthily and balanced?

2. Consider the impact of consuming news and information in your life. Journal how to establish healthy boundaries and practices to ensure you are grounded in truth amidst the noise of news.

Key Lessons:

1. Discerning News versus Truth: Reflect on the importance of discerning between news and truth. Explore how media narratives, biases, and agendas influence our perception and understanding of events.

2. Guarding Your Mind and Heart: Contemplate the significance of guarding your mind and heart from consuming excessive news and information. Reflect on the potential negative impact it can have on your mental health, emotions, and overall well-being.

3. Seeking Truth and Wisdom: Explore the importance of seeking truth and wisdom beyond the news. Reflect on how grounding yourself in God's Word, seeking diverse perspectives, and engaging in critical thinking can lead to a more balanced and informed understanding of the world.

Self-Reflection Questions:

1. Reflect on a recent news story or information that has affected you emotionally or mentally. How did it impact your thoughts and feelings? How can you discern between news and truth to process and respond healthily and balanced?

_____

_____

_____

_____

_____

_____

2. Understand the potential influence of media narratives, biases, and agendas on our perception of events. How can you cultivate a discerning mind to interpret news and information accurately and critically?

_____

_____

_____

_____

_____

_____

3. Contemplate the impact of consuming excessive news and information. How does it affect your mental health, emotions, and overall well-being? What boundaries and practices can you establish to ensure a healthier relationship with the news?

_____

_____

_____

_____

_____

_____

4. Reflect on the importance of seeking truth beyond the news. How can you ground yourself in God's Word and rely on His wisdom to better understand the world? How can you actively seek diverse

perspectives to broaden your knowledge and outlook?

_____

_____

_____

_____

_____

_____

5. Explore the role of critical thinking in discerning news versus truth. How can you enhance your critical thinking skills to navigate information overload and separate fact from opinion? What resources or strategies can you utilize to develop a more informed perspective?

_____

_____

_____

_____

When Joy Feels So Very Unrealistic

Journaling Prompts:

1. Reflect on a time when you struggled to experience joy in a challenging season of life—Journal about the obstacles or beliefs that made joy feel unrealistic or unattainable. Explore ways in which you can redefine joy in your life.

2. Consider the impact of gratitude on your ability to experience joy—journal about moments or blessings that bring you joy and how practicing gratitude can amplify those feelings.

Key Lessons:

1. Navigating Unrealistic Expectations: Reflect on the challenges of feeling joy when faced with difficult circumstances or unrealistic expectations. Explore the importance of acknowledging and accepting the reality of your situation while finding hope and joy within it.

2. Cultivating Joy amid Challenges: Contemplate the power of intentional action to cultivate joy. Reflect on practical strategies such as practicing gratitude, seeking moments of delight, and finding solace in God's presence that can help bring joy even during challenging circumstances.

3. Embracing the Ebb and Flow of Joy: Explore embracing joy and sorrow as part of the human experience. Reflect on how joy can coexist alongside pain, grief, and uncertainty and how finding meaning and Purpose in those moments can lead to deeper and lasting joy.

Self-Reflection Questions:

1. Think about a time when you struggled to experience joy in a challenging season of life. What obstacles or beliefs made joy feel unrealistic or unattainable? How can you redefine joy in your life to make it more accessible and meaningful?

_____

_____

_____

_____

_____

_____

2. Reflect on the impact of gratitude on your ability to experience joy. What specific moments or blessings in your life bring you joy? How can you practice gratitude to amplify those feelings and cultivate a deeper sense of joy?

_____

_____

_____

_____

_____

_____

3. Contemplate the challenges of feeling joy when faced with difficult circumstances or unrealistic expectations. How can you find hope and joy within your reality? What steps can you take to acknowledge and accept your situation while still seeking joy?

_____

_____

_____

_____

_____

_____

4. Explore practical strategies to cultivate joy during challenges. How can you incorporate practices such as gratitude, seeking moments of delight, and finding solace in God's presence into your daily life? What

other activities or habits can help bring joy even in difficult times?

_____

_____

_____

_____

_____

_____

5. Reflect on the concept of embracing both joy and sorrow as part of the human experience. How can you find meaning and Purpose in pain, grief, and uncertainty? How does embracing the ebb and flow of joy contribute to a deeper and lasting sense of joy in your life?

_____

_____

_____

_____

When Joy Feels So Very Unrealistic

Journaling Prompts:

1. Reflect on a challenging situation in your life where joy feels unrealistic or out of reach. Journal about the specific emotions and beliefs that accompany this experience. How can you open yourself up to finding joy even during your circumstances?

2. Consider moments when you have experienced unexpected joy or delight. Journal about those instances and reflect on what contributed to those joyful experiences. How can you intentionally create more of those moments in your life?

Key Lessons:

1. Redefining Joy: Reflect on how joy can be redefined in challenging circumstances. Explore the idea that joy does not always mean a lack of suffering but rather a deep-seated sense of peace, contentment, and gratitude despite the hardships.

2. Choosing Joy: Contemplate the power of choice in experiencing joy. Recognize that joy is not solely dependent on external factors but a conscious decision to find beauty, gratitude, and hope in every situation.

3. Finding Joy in the Present: Explore the importance of mindfulness and living in the present moment as a pathway to experiencing joy. Reflect on how you can cultivate a mindset of presence, gratitude, and awareness to embrace daily joy.

Self-Reflection Questions:

1. Think about a challenging situation in your life where joy feels unrealistic or out of reach. What specific emotions and beliefs accompany this experience? How can you open yourself up to finding joy even amidst your circumstances?

_____

_____

_____

_____

_____

_____

2. Reflect on how joy can be redefined in challenging circumstances. How would you redefine joy for yourself? How can you cultivate peace, contentment, and gratitude despite hardships?

_____

_____

_____

_____

_____

_____

3. Contemplate the power of choice in experiencing joy. How can you consciously choose joy in your life? What practices or habits can you develop to find beauty, gratitude, and hope even amid difficulties?

_____

_____

_____

_____

_____

_____

4. Explore the importance of mindfulness and living in the present moment as a pathway to experiencing joy. How can you cultivate a daily mindset of presence, gratitude, and awareness? In what ways can practicing mindfulness help you embrace joy each day?

_____

_____

_____

_____

_____

_____

5. Reflect on moments when you have experienced unexpected joy or delight. What factors contributed to those joyful experiences? How can you intentionally create more of those moments in your life? What activities, people, or practices bring you joy, and how can you incorporate them into your routine?

_____

_____

_____

_____

_____

_____

Why Would You Let This Happen, God?

Journaling Prompts:

1. Reflect on a challenging or painful experience where you questioned why God allowed it to happen. Journal about your feelings, doubts, and thoughts surrounding this event. How can you find peace or understanding amid your unanswered questions?

2. Consider times when you have witnessed or experienced unexpected beauty or redemption in the aftermath of difficult circumstances. Journal about those instances and reflect on how they have shaped your faith or perspective. How can you hold onto hope and trust God's goodness despite the unanswered "why" questions?

Key Lessons:

1. Wrestling with Unanswered Questions: Reflect on grappling with unanswered "why" questions in the face of pain or hardship. Explore the idea that it is normal and okay to question, doubt, and seek understanding, even if the answers may not be readily available.

2. Embracing God's Mysterious Ways: Contemplate surrendering control and trusting in God's sovereignty when things don't go as planned. Reflect on how surrendering your "why" questions can lead to a deeper reliance on faith and a greater sense of peace.

3. Finding Beauty and Purpose in the Unexpected: Explore the notion that beauty and Purpose can emerge from difficult and painful situations. Reflect on how God can redeem and transform brokenness and how you can actively seek glimpses of beauty and signs of God's presence amid hardship.

Self-Reflection Questions:

1. Think about a challenging or painful experience where you questioned why God allowed it to happen. What were your feelings, doubts, and thoughts surrounding this event? How can you find peace or understanding amid your unanswered questions?

_____

_____

_____

_____

_____

_____

2. Reflect on grappling with unanswered "why" questions in the face of pain or hardship. How comfortable are you with questioning, doubting, and seeking understanding? How can you navigate these questions healthily and constructively?

_____

_____

_____

_____

_____

_____

3. Contemplate surrendering control and trusting in God's sovereignty. How can you relinquish the need for immediate answers and surrender your "why" questions to God? What practices or habits can help deepen your reliance on faith and find peace amid uncertainty?

_____

_____

_____

_____

_____

_____

4. Explore the notion of finding beauty and Purpose in unexpected places. Can you think of instances where beauty or redemption emerged from a difficult

situation? How did those experiences shape your faith or perspective? How can you actively seek glimpses of beauty and signs of God's presence amid hardship?

_____

_____

_____

_____

_____

_____

5. Reflect on the role of hope and trust in God's goodness despite the unanswered "why" questions. How can you hold onto hope, even when facing circumstances challenging your faith? How can you strengthen your trust in God's plan and Purpose for your life, even when you don't have all the answers?

_____

_____

_____

Step After Step of Unwavering Obedience

Journaling Prompts:

1. Reflect on a time in your life when you faced a decision requiring unwavering obedience. Journal about the challenges, doubts, and fears you experienced. How did your obedience contribute to growth, transformation, or unexpected blessings?

2. Consider moments when you have witnessed or experienced the fruit of unwavering obedience in your life or the lives of others. Journal about those instances and reflect on how they impacted your faith or your understanding of God's faithfulness. How can you cultivate a greater willingness to obey, even when it feels difficult or uncertain?

Key Lessons:

1. The Cost and Reward of Obedience: Reflect on unwavering obedience and the challenges it may present. Explore that obedience often requires sacrifices, stepping out of comfort zones, or surrendering personal desires. Reflect on the rewards and blessings from wholehearted obedience to God's plans and purposes.

2. Trusting God's Guidance: Contemplate the importance of trusting God's guidance, even when the path is unclear or different from our expectations. Reflect on the faith and surrender required to follow God's lead and how our obedience can align us with His perfect will for our lives.

3. The Power of Stepping Out: Explore the notion that taking one step after another in unwavering obedience can lead to transformation and growth. Reflect on the potential ripple effects of our

obedience on ourselves, others, and the broader narrative of God's redemption in the world.

Self-Reflection Questions:

1. Think about a time in your life when you faced a decision requiring unwavering obedience. What challenges, doubts, and fears did you experience during that time? How did your obedience contribute to growth, transformation, or unexpected blessings?

_____

_____

_____

_____

_____

_____

2. Reflect on unwavering obedience and the sacrifices it may require. Are there areas in your life where you struggle to surrender or obey fully? What steps can you take to cultivate a greater willingness to obey, even when it feels difficult or uncertain?

_____

_____

_____

_____

_____

_____

3. Contemplate the importance of trusting God's guidance, even when the path is unclear or different from your expectations. How strong is your trust in God's wisdom and plans for your life? In what ways can you deepen your faith and surrender to His guidance?

_____

_____

_____

_____

_____

_____

4. Explore stepping out in unwavering obedience and the potential for transformation and growth. Can you think of instances in your life where your obedience

led to positive changes or had ripple effects on others? How can you continue to take one step after another in obedience to God's calling?

_____

_____

_____

_____

_____

_____

5. Reflect on the rewards and blessings that can come from wholehearted obedience to God's plans and purposes. How have you experienced the rewards of obedience in your life? How does your understanding of the potential blessings impact your willingness to obey, even in challenging circumstances?

_____

_____

_____

_____

65

Three Questions to Ask Before Giving a Response You Can't Take Back

Journaling Prompts:

1. Reflect on a time when you responded that you later regretted. Journal about the circumstances, emotions, and consequences of that situation. What factors led you to give a hasty or thoughtless response? How can you learn from that experience and approach similar situations more intentionally in the future?

2. Consider a recent interaction where you had to decide or respond to a challenging situation. Journal the questions you asked yourself before giving a response. How did those questions shape your perspective and affect the outcome of the situation? How can you incorporate a thoughtful and intentional approach in your future responses?

Key Lessons:

1. The Power of Pausing: Reflect on pausing and taking time before responding. Explore the idea that pausing allows for reflection, self-control, and a more thoughtful and measured approach to communication. Reflect on the importance of resisting the urge to react impulsively.

2. The Art of Asking Questions: Contemplate the role of insightful questioning in shaping our responses. Reflect on the impact of asking clarifying questions to gain understanding before giving a response. Consider how asking questions fosters empathy, promotes better communication, and leads to more effective problem-solving.

3. Reducing Regret: Explore the notion that we can prevent unnecessary regret by considering the potential consequences of our responses before speaking. Reflect on how proactive reflection and self-awareness can help us align our words with our

values, avoid hurtful or damaging communication, and cultivate healthier relationships.

Self-Reflection Questions:

1. Think about a time when you gave a response that you later regretted. What were the circumstances, emotions, and consequences of that situation? What factors led you to give a hasty or thoughtless response? How can you learn from that experience and approach similar situations more intentionally in the future?

_____

_____

_____

_____

_____

_____

2. Reflect on the significance of pausing and taking time before giving a response. How comfortable are you with pausing before speaking? How can you cultivate the habit of pausing, even in challenging or high-pressure situations? What strategies or

techniques can help you resist the urge to react impulsively?

_____

_____

_____

_____

_____

_____

3. Contemplate the role of insightful questioning in shaping your responses. How often do you ask clarifying questions to gain understanding before giving a response? How can incorporating this practice improve your communication and relationships? What are some examples of questions you can ask to foster empathy and promote effective problem-solving?

_____

_____

_____

_____

_____

_____

4. Explore the notion of reducing regret by considering the potential consequences of your responses before speaking. How can proactive reflection and self-awareness help you align your words with your values? How can this practice contribute to healthier relationships and more effective communication?

_____

_____

_____

_____

_____

_____

5. Reflect on the impact of intentional and thoughtful responses in your interactions and relationships. How have you experienced the benefits of pausing,

asking questions, and considering consequences before speaking? How can you continue to prioritize these practices in your communication moving forward?

_____

_____

_____

_____

_____

_____

Is It Really That Big of a Deal If I Stay Offended?

Journaling Prompts:

1. Reflect on a time when you held onto offense or grudges. Journal about the circumstances, emotions, and experiences surrounding that offense. How did staying offended impact your mindset, relationships, and overall well-being? What steps can you take to release that offense and find healing?

2. Consider instances where you let go of offense and forgive. Journal about the process of forgiveness and its effects on your heart and mindset. How did choosing to release offense bring freedom and restoration to your life? How can you cultivate a heart of forgiveness in your daily interactions?

Key Lessons:

1. The Chains of Offense: Reflect on the weight and burden of holding onto offense. Explore the idea that staying offended can hinder personal growth, damage relationships, and block the process of healing and redemption. Reflect on the negative consequences of choosing to stay offended.

2. The Power of Forgiveness: Contemplate the transformative power of choosing forgiveness. Reflect on how releasing offense can bring freedom, peace, and restoration to your life. Explore the idea that forgiveness is not about excusing the actions of others but about choosing to let go of the pain and freeing yourself from bitterness.

Self-Reflection Questions:

1. Think about a time when you held onto offense or grudges. What were the circumstances, emotions, and experiences surrounding that offense? How did staying offended impact your mindset, relationships, and overall well-being? How can you take steps to release that offense and find healing?

_____

_____

_____

_____

_____

_____

2. Reflect on the weight and burden of holding onto offense. How does staying offended hinder personal growth and damage relationships? What negative consequences have you experienced from choosing to stay offended? How can you let go of offense and its associated chains?

_____

_____

_____

_____

_____

_____

3. Contemplate the power of choosing forgiveness. Can you recall instances where you let go of offense and forgive? How did that process bring freedom and restoration to your life? How can you cultivate a heart of forgiveness in your daily interactions and relationships?

_____

_____

_____

_____

_____

_____

4. Explore the idea that forgiveness is not about excusing the actions of others but about choosing to let go of the pain and freeing yourself from bitterness. How do you personally define forgiveness? How can you shift your perspective on forgiveness to focus on your own well-being and inner healing rather than dwelling on the wrongs done to you?

_____

_____

_____

_____

_____

_____

5. Reflect on how forgiveness can transform and restore your life. How has forgiveness impacted your own heart and mindset? In what areas of your life do you hold onto offense, and how can you actively choose forgiveness to experience personal freedom and growth?

This Won't Be For Nothing

Journaling Prompts:

1. Reflect on a difficult experience or season that felt purposeless or meaningless. Journal about the emotions, struggles, and questions you wrestled with. How did you discover beauty, redemption, or Purpose in that situation? What lessons or growth did you experience as a result?

2. Consider moments when you witnessed or experienced the impact of your past struggles or pain on others. Journal about those instances and reflect on how your story, despite its challenges, has brought hope or encouragement to others. How can you continue to find meaning and Purpose in sharing your story?

Key Lessons:

1. Embracing the Bigger Picture: Reflect on the idea that our difficult experiences and trials are often

81

connected to a greater purpose. Explore the concept that our pain can be redeemed and used for something meaningful, both in our own lives and in the lives of others. Reflect on the hope that comes from embracing the bigger picture beyond our immediate circumstances.

2. Finding Purpose in Sharing our Stories: Contemplate the power of sharing our stories with vulnerability and authenticity. Reflect on our stories' impact on others, bringing encouragement, empathy, and a sense of connection. Explore how finding Purpose in sharing our stories allows us to find beauty and meaning in our past pain or struggles.

Self-Reflection Questions:

1. Think about a difficult experience or season that initially felt purposeless or without meaning. What emotions, struggles, and questions did you wrestle with then? How did you discover beauty, redemption, or Purpose in that situation? What lessons or growth did you experience as a result?

_____

_____

_____

_____

_____

_____

2. Reflect on the idea that our difficult experiences and trials are often connected to a greater purpose. How does embracing the bigger picture beyond your immediate circumstances bring hope and perspective? In what ways have you experienced the

redemption of your pain or challenges leading to a greater purpose in your life?

_____

_____

_____

_____

_____

_____

3. Contemplate the power of sharing your story with vulnerability and authenticity. How comfortable are you with sharing your own experiences? How have you witnessed or experienced the impact of sharing stories with others? How can you cultivate a deeper sense of Purpose in sharing your story?

_____

_____

_____

_____

_____

_____

4. Explore finding Purpose and meaning in sharing your story. How does finding Purpose in sharing your story allow you to find beauty and meaning in your past pain or struggles? How can you continue to share your story to bring hope and encouragement to others?

_____

_____

_____

_____

_____

_____

5. Reflect on the potential impact your story can have on others. How have you witnessed or experienced your past struggles or pain bringing hope or encouragement to others? How can you continue to

find meaning and Purpose in sharing your story, knowing it can inspire and bring healing to others?

_____

_____

_____

_____

_____

_____

The Only Love That Never Fails

Journaling Prompts:

1. Reflect on when you experienced or witnessed an example of love that never fails. Journal about the circumstances, emotions, and impact of that experience. How did it shape your understanding of love and its enduring nature? How can you incorporate that understanding into your relationships and interactions?

2. Consider moments when you struggled to show unconditional love or experienced challenges in offering love that never fails. Journal about those instances and reflect on the lessons you learned from those experiences. How can you cultivate a deeper capacity to love unconditionally in your relationships and daily life?

Key Lessons:

1. Unconditional Love's Source: Reflect on the understanding that the only love that never fails comes from God. Contemplate the idea that God's love is a constant, unwavering, and sacrificial love that serves as a model for our relationships. Reflect on the significance of relying on God's love and seeking His guidance to love others well.

2. Embracing Love's Imperfections: Explore the notion that love is not always perfect or without challenges. Reflect on the acceptance and grace required in navigating the imperfections and difficulties of love. Consider the lessons learned from embracing love's imperfections and applying forgiveness, humility, and patience in our relationships.

Self-Reflection Questions:

1. Think about a time when you experienced or witnessed an example of love that never fails. What were the circumstances, emotions, and impact of that experience? How did it shape your understanding of love and its enduring nature? How can you incorporate that understanding into your relationships and interactions?

_____

_____

_____

_____

_____

_____

2. Reflect on the understanding that the only love that never fails comes from God. How has relying on God's love influenced the way you love others? In what areas of your life can you seek God's guidance

and cultivate a deeper capacity to love unconditionally?

_____

_____

_____

_____

_____

_____

3. Contemplate that love is not always perfect or without challenges. Can you recall instances where you struggled to show unconditional love or experienced challenges in offering love that never fails? What were the lessons you learned from those experiences? How can you apply forgiveness, humility, and patience in navigating the imperfections and difficulties of love?

_____

_____

_____

_____

_____

_____

4. Explore the notion of accepting and embracing love's imperfections. How comfortable are you with accepting and extending grace in your relationships? How can you practice forgiveness and humility to strengthen your ability to love unconditionally?

_____

_____

_____

_____

_____

_____

5. Reflect on the impact of unconditional love in your own life. How has experiencing or witnessing unconditional love shaped your perspective and relationships? How can you intentionally nurture a

loving and selfless mindset in daily interactions and relationships?

_____

_____

_____

_____

_____

_____

When I Deny Jesus

Journaling Prompts:

1. Reflect on when you felt pressured to deny or compromise your faith in Jesus. Journal about the circumstances, emotions, and inner struggles you faced. How did you handle the situation? What were the consequences and lessons you learned from that experience? How can you grow in your faith and commitment to Jesus moving forward?

2. Consider moments when you witnessed or heard stories of others denying Jesus. Journal about those stories' impact on you and the questions they raised. How do these stories challenge or inspire your commitment to Jesus? How can you strengthen your resolve to stand firm in your faith, even when faced with opposition or pressure?

Key Lessons:

1. The Cost of Denying Jesus: Reflect on the significance and consequences of denying Jesus in various aspects of life. Explore how it can impact our relationship with God, our sense of identity, and our witness to others. Reflect on the importance of standing firm in our faith, even when faced with challenges or opposition.

2. Embracing Courage and Conviction: Contemplate the need for courage and conviction to stand up for our faith. Reflect on the examples of individuals who have demonstrated unwavering commitment to Jesus, even in adversity. Explore the idea that our faith in Jesus requires boldness and a willingness to prioritize Him above all else.

Self-Reflection Questions:

1. Think about when you felt pressured to deny or compromise your faith in Jesus. What were your circumstances, emotions, and inner struggles during that time? How did you handle the situation? What were the consequences and lessons you learned from that experience? How can you grow in your faith and commitment to Jesus moving forward?

_____

_____

_____

_____

_____

_____

2. Reflect on the significance and consequences of denying Jesus in various aspects of life. How does denying Jesus impact your relationship with God, sense of identity, and witness to others? How can you

prioritize Jesus and stand firm in your faith, even when faced with challenges or opposition?

_____

_____

_____

_____

_____

_____

3. Contemplate the need for courage and conviction in standing up for your faith. Can you recall examples of individuals who have demonstrated unwavering commitment to Jesus, even in the face of adversity? How does their example inspire you to embrace courage and conviction in your faith journey?

_____

_____

_____

_____

_____

_____

4. Explore the idea that our faith in Jesus requires boldness and a willingness to prioritize Him above all else. How comfortable are you with prioritizing Jesus in all aspects of your life? In what areas do you struggle to stand firm in your faith? How can you cultivate a deeper conviction and firm commitment to Jesus?

_____

_____

_____

_____

_____

_____

5. Reflect on the lessons learned from stories of others denying Jesus. How do these stories challenge or inspire your commitment to Jesus? How can you strengthen your resolve to stand firm in your faith,

even when faced with opposition or pressure? How can you actively support and encourage others on their faith journey?

_____

_____

_____

_____

_____

_____

Three Perspectives to Remember When Your Normal Gets Hijacked

Journaling Prompts:

1. Reflect on a time when a significant event or circumstance disrupted your normal life. Journal about the emotions, challenges, and uncertainties you experienced. How did it feel to have your normal routine or expectations hijacked? What did you learn about yourself, your resilience, and your ability to adapt?

2. Consider moments when you could shift your perspective and find beauty or redemption amid a hijacked normal. Journal about those instances and reflect on the lessons you learned from them. How can you apply those lessons to future challenges and disruptions?

Key Lessons:

1. The Power of Perspective: Reflect on the importance of maintaining a healthy perspective when our normal gets hijacked. Explore how shifting our perspective can help us find beauty, growth, and new possibilities during challenging circumstances. Reflect on the significance of choosing gratitude, hope, and resilience in navigating disruptions.

2. Embracing Adaptability and Resilience: Contemplate the ability to adapt and be resilient in the face of a hijacked normal. Reflect on the lessons learned from times when you had to adjust to unexpected changes. Explore how cultivating adaptability and resilience can help you navigate future disruptions and find strength in challenging seasons.

Self-Reflection Questions:

1. Think about a time when a significant event or circumstance disrupted your normal life. What were the emotions, challenges, and uncertainties you experienced during that time? How did it feel to have your normal routine or expectations hijacked? What did you learn about yourself, your resilience, and your ability to adapt?

_____

_____

_____

_____

_____

_____

2. Reflect on the importance of maintaining a healthy perspective when your normal gets hijacked. How has shifted your perspective helped you find beauty, growth, and new possibilities amid challenging circumstances? How can you embrace gratitude,

hope, and resilience to navigate disruptions and maintain a positive perspective?

_____

_____

_____

_____

_____

_____

3. Contemplate the ability to adapt and be resilient in the face of a hijacked normal. Can you recall instances when you had to adjust to unexpected changes? What were the lessons you learned from those experiences? How can you cultivate adaptability and resilience to help you navigate future disruptions and find strength in challenging seasons?

_____

_____

_____

_____

_____

_____

4. Explore finding beauty and redemption amid a hijacked normal. How comfortable are you with seeking and recognizing the beauty or growth that can emerge from difficult circumstances? How can you open yourself to new possibilities and positive outcomes, even during disruptions?

_____

_____

_____

_____

_____

_____

5. Reflect on your personal growth and resilience in past disruptions. How have those experiences shaped who you are today? How can you draw on those

lessons and strengths to face future challenges and disruptions with confidence and grace?

_____

_____

_____

_____

_____

_____

Saved by Suffering

Journaling Prompts:

1. Reflect on when you experienced suffering or hardship that ultimately led to growth or transformation. Journal about the emotions, struggles, and lessons learned during that time. How has that experience shaped your understanding of suffering and its potential for redemption? In what ways can you find beauty and growth during your current challenges?

2. Consider moments when you witnessed or heard stories of others who found salvation or redemption through their suffering. Journal about those instances and reflect on those stories' impact on you. How did they inspire or encourage you in your journey? How can you apply their lessons and perspectives to find hope and Purpose in your suffering?

Key Lessons:

1. The Transformative Power of Suffering: Reflect on the idea that suffering can catalyze growth, transformation, and redemption. Contemplate the lessons and insights that can emerge from periods of hardship. Explore the potential to develop resilience, empathy, and a deeper dependence on God through suffering.

2. Finding Purpose and Meaning in Suffering: Contemplate the notion that suffering can be an opportunity to discover Purpose and meaning in our lives. Reflect on how suffering can refine our values, priorities, and relationships. Explore using our experiences of suffering to bring comfort, support, and hope to others.

Self-Reflection Questions:

1. Think about a time when you experienced suffering or hardship that ultimately led to growth or transformation. What were the emotions, struggles, and lessons learned during that time? How has that experience shaped your understanding of suffering and its potential for redemption? In what ways can you find beauty and growth amid your current challenges?

_____

_____

_____

_____

_____

_____

2. Reflect on the idea that suffering can catalyze growth, transformation, and redemption. Can you recall moments of insight or personal growth that emerged from periods of suffering? How has

suffering shaped you and deepened your empathy towards others? How can you seek resilience, reliance on God, and a sense of Purpose amid your current or future suffering?

_____

_____

_____

_____

_____

_____

3. Contemplate the notion that suffering can be an opportunity to discover Purpose and meaning in our lives. How has suffering refined your values, priorities, or relationships? How can your experiences of suffering be used to bring comfort, support, and hope to others going through similar challenges?

_____

_____

_____

_____

_____

_____

4. Explore how your perspective on suffering has evolved. How have you grown in finding meaning and Purpose in difficult circumstances? How can you actively seek opportunities to learn and grow from your suffering rather than allowing it to define or defeat you?

_____

_____

_____

_____

_____

_____

5. Reflect on the lessons and insights gained from stories of others who found salvation or redemption through their suffering. How did those stories inspire

or encourage you? What lessons or perspectives can you apply to find hope, Purpose, and beauty in your suffering?

_____

_____

_____

_____

_____

_____

Sometimes It's a One- or Two-Verse Day

Journaling Prompts:

1. Reflect on a time when you found deep meaning, comfort, or guidance in a single verse or a short passage from the Bible. Journal about the circumstances surrounding that experience, your emotions, and their impact on your perspective or actions. How did that one or two verses provide clarity or strength in that particular season of your life? What lessons can you carry from that experience to help you find solace or inspiration during challenging times?

2. Consider moments when you struggled to engage with longer passages or extensive study of the Bible. Journal about the obstacles or reasons behind that difficulty, exploring any frustrations or doubts you experienced. How can you approach those moments with grace and compassion for yourself? How can

you embrace the idea of finding beauty and wisdom even in a single verse or a concise portion of Scripture?

Key Lessons:

1. The Power of Concise Truth: Reflect on the impact of one or two verses on our lives. Explore how a brief encounter with God's Word can provide profound insights, encouragement, or guidance. Reflect on cherishing and meditating on even the smallest portions of Scripture.

2. Embracing Simplicity and Accessibility: Contemplate the idea that our engagement with Scripture doesn't always have to be complex or overwhelming. Reflect on the importance of finding Bible study approaches that resonate with our individual needs and capacities. Embrace the concept of meeting God wherever we are, even if it means focusing on a single verse or a short passage.

Self-Reflection Questions:

1. Think about a time when you found deep meaning, comfort, or guidance in a single verse or a short passage from the Bible. What were the circumstances surrounding that experience? How did it impact your perspective or actions in that particular season of your life? How can you use that experience's lessons and insights to help you find solace or inspiration during challenging times?

_____

_____

_____

_____

_____

_____

2. Reflect on the impact of one or two verses on our lives. Can you recall instances when a brief encounter with God's Word provided profound insights, encouragement, or guidance? How did those concise

truths shape your thinking or choices? How can you cherish and meditate on even the smallest portions of Scripture in your daily life?

_____

_____

_____

_____

_____

_____

3. Contemplate the barriers or reasons that may sometimes make it difficult for you to engage with longer passages or extensive study of the Bible. What obstacles or frustrations have you encountered in such situations? How can you approach those moments with grace and compassion for yourself? How can you embrace the beauty and wisdom found even in a single verse or a concise portion of Scripture?

_____

_____

_____

_____

_____

_____

4. Explore the idea of simplicity and accessibility in our engagement with Scripture. How comfortable are you with finding Bible study approaches that resonate with your individual needs and capacities? How can you create a space for meeting God amid your limitations, even if it means focusing on a single verse or a short passage?

_____

_____

_____

_____

_____

_____

5. Reflect on how your understanding and appreciation of the Bible have evolved. How have you grown in your ability to find meaning and application in both longer passages and the smallest snippets of Scripture? How can you continue to cultivate a deep love and reverence for God's Word, regardless of its length or complexity?

_____

_____

_____

_____

_____

_____

When Things Get Worse Just Before They Get Better

Journaling Prompts:

1. Reflect on a time in your life when things worsened before they got better. What challenges did you face during that time? How did you navigate through the difficulties and find hope?

2. Consider a current situation in your life where things might be getting worse. How can you approach this situation with a perspective of hope and trust that things will eventually get better?

Key Lessons:

1. The paradox of struggle: Understand that sometimes, things may appear to be worsening before they improve. Recognize that growth and transformation often occur through challenges and difficulties.

2. Navigating the "in-between": Learn to navigate the "in-between" seasons when there is no resolution. Embrace patience, trust, and personal growth opportunities during these times.

3. Holding onto hope: Emphasize the importance of holding onto hope, even during challenging circumstances. Remember that better days are possible, and God works behind the scenes for our good.

Self-Reflection Questions:

1. Can you think of a time when you faced a difficult season that appeared to be worsening before it got better? How did you find hope and strength during that time?

_____

_____

_____

_____

_____

2. How do you typically respond when things seem to be getting worse? Are there any patterns of thinking or behaviors you notice during these times of hardship?

_____

_____

_____

_____

_____

_____

3. Reflect on the "in-between" seasons in your life. How have you navigated these times in the past? In what ways can you embrace the opportunity for personal growth and trust in God's plan amid uncertainty?

_____

_____

_____

_____

_____

_____

4. Consider a current situation in your life where things might be getting worse. How can you consciously hold onto hope and trust that better days are ahead?

_____

_____

_____

_____

_____

_____

5. Reflect on your understanding of God's faithfulness and ability to work in challenging circumstances. How does this perspective influence your ability to hold onto hope even when things seem to be getting worse?

_____

_____

_____

_____

_____

_____

The Blessings of Boundaries

Journaling Prompts:

1. Reflect on a specific area where you struggle to set boundaries. What are the reasons behind this difficulty? How would your life be improved if you could establish healthy boundaries in that area?

2. Write about a time when you set a boundary and experienced its positive impact on your life. How did it change your relationships, well-being, or overall sense of peace?

Key Lessons:

1. The importance of boundaries: Recognize the significance of establishing boundaries in various areas of life, such as relationships, work, and personal well-being. Understand that boundaries are essential for maintaining healthy and balanced lives.

2. Self-worth and boundaries: Learn that setting healthy boundaries is an act of self-respect and self-care. Understand that when you establish and enforce boundaries, you value yourself and create space for your needs and values.

3. Navigating guilt and criticism: Explore how to handle feelings of guilt or criticism when setting boundaries. Understand that it is normal to encounter resistance or pushback, but maintaining your boundaries is vital for your overall well-being.

Self-Reflection Questions:

1. Consider the areas where you struggle to set boundaries. What underlying fears or beliefs might be contributing to this struggle? How do these boundaries affect your overall well-being?

_____

_____

_____

_____

_____

2. Reflect on when you set a boundary and faced resistance or criticism. How did you handle these reactions? In hindsight, would you have done anything differently?

_____

_____

_____

_____

_____

_____

3. Explore your understanding of self-worth and how it relates to setting boundaries. How can establishing and enforcing boundaries reflect your self-respect and value?

_____

_____

_____

_____

_____

_____

4. Consider a relationship or situation where setting boundaries could greatly benefit your emotional, mental, or physical health. How can you approach setting these boundaries lovingly and assertively?

_____

_____

_____

_____

_____

_____

5. Reflect on any guilt or self-doubt that arises when setting boundaries. What can you do to remind yourself that boundaries are important and necessary for your well-being, even if they may temporarily upset others?

_____

_____

_____

_____

_____

_____

Where Is My Happily Ever After?

Journaling Prompts:

1. Reflect on a specific expectation or idea of a "happily ever after" you held onto. How has this expectation impacted your life and relationships? How can you shift your perspective to find beauty in unexpected places or outcomes?

2. Consider a time when you experienced disappointment because your circumstances didn't align with your desired "happily ever after." How did you navigate through that season? What did you learn about yourself and your faith?

Key Lessons:

1. The illusion of a perfect ending: Recognize that life rarely unfolds as we envision it, and pursuing a "happily ever after" can lead to disappointment and missed opportunities for growth and beauty.

2. Embracing the present moment: Learn to find beauty and joy in the present, even if it doesn't align with your expectations or desires. Emphasize the importance of gratitude and contentment, cultivating a mindset of appreciation for the blessings in your life right now.

3. Surrender and trust: Understand the importance of surrendering your desires and dreams to God, trusting His plan even when it diverges from your own. Recognize that true fulfillment comes from aligning your desires with God's purposes and trusting Him.

Self-Reflection Questions:

1. Reflect on a specific "happily ever after" you were hoping for that didn't come to fruition. How did this experience impact you emotionally and spiritually? Have you been able to find beauty or Purpose in the unexpected outcome?

_____

_____

_____

_____

_____

_____

2. Consider how your expectations of a perfect ending have influenced your relationships and interactions with others. Can you make any adjustments to foster more realistic and compassionate perspectives?

_____

_____

_____

_____

_____

_____

3. Reflect on a moment when you found beauty or joy in an unexpected outcome or circumstance. How did being present and cultivating gratitude enhance your experience? How can you incorporate this mindset in other areas of your life?

_____

_____

_____

_____

_____

_____

4. How comfortable are you surrendering your desires and dreams to God's plan? Reflect on any resistances or fears you may have. What steps can you take to cultivate a greater trust in God's guidance and timing?

_____

_____

_____

_____

_____

_____

5. Consider your current mindset regarding a "happily ever after." Are there any adjustments you can make to foster contentment in the present while still pursuing your goals and dreams? How can you align your desires with God's purposes for your life?

_____

_____

_____

_____

_____

_____

134

When Giving Grace Feels Hard

Journaling Prompts:

1. Reflect on a situation or person where extending grace feels particularly challenging. What factors contribute to the difficulty? How can you approach this situation with empathy and grace?

2. Write about when someone extended grace to you even though you didn't deserve it. How did that act of grace impact you? How can you apply the lessons learned from that experience to extend grace to others?

Key Lessons:

1. Choosing grace: Understand the importance of extending grace to others, even when it feels difficult. Recognize that grace is a powerful tool for healing and reconciliation in relationships.

2. Empathy and understanding: Cultivate empathy and a deeper understanding of others' perspectives and experiences. Recognize that everyone has unique stories and struggles, which can help cultivate compassion and grace.

3. Releasing the need for control: Learn to release the need for control and accept that you cannot change or control others. Focus on your attitude, actions, and responses, and extend grace without expecting anything in return.

Self-Reflection Questions:

1. Reflect on when you found it challenging to extend grace to someone. What were the underlying reasons for this difficulty? How can you shift your perspective or cultivate empathy to make grace more accessible in that situation?

_____

_____

_____

_____

_____

_____

2. Think about an experience when someone gave you grace when you didn't deserve it. How did that act of grace impact your relationship? How can you apply the lessons learned from that experience to extend grace to others?

_____

_____

_____

_____

_____

_____

3. Consider your general approach to conflicts or disagreements. Do you tend to default to a grace-filled or more judgmental response? What steps can you take to cultivate a mindset of grace in your interactions with others, especially in difficult moments?

_____

_____

_____

_____

_____

_____

4. Reflect on your need for control in relationships. Are there situations or people where you struggle to let go of control? How does this need for control

hinder your ability to extend grace? What practices can you implement to release this need and focus on extending grace instead?

_____

_____

_____

_____

_____

_____

5. Reflect on a relationship or situation where extending grace is hard. Can you identify any underlying assumptions or expectations that challenge your ability to show grace? How can you reframe your mindset and approach to foster a more grace-filled response?

_____

_____

_____

_____

Forgiveness: The Double-Edged Word

Journaling Prompts:

1. Reflect on a situation where forgiveness feels particularly challenging. Explore your emotions, thoughts, and any barriers to forgiveness that you may be experiencing. How can you begin to release the burden of unforgiveness and find healing?

2. Consider when you experienced the power of forgiveness in your life. How did it impact your well-being and relationships? How can you extend that same forgiveness to others?

Key Lessons:

1. The complexities of forgiveness: Understand that forgiveness is complex and multifaceted. Recognize that it is not about condoning or forgetting the

offense but rather about releasing the negative emotions and consequences of the hurt.

2. The healing power of forgiveness: Learn about the transformative power of forgiveness in one's own life. Understand that forgiveness is not just for the offender's benefit but also for the forgiver's personal healing, freedom, and growth.

3. The ongoing journey of forgiveness: Embrace forgiveness as a journey that takes time and commitment. Recognize that forgiveness may need to be extended multiple times and require ongoing work to heal fully.

Self-Reflection Questions:

1. Reflect on a grudge or past hurt that you have been holding onto. What emotions and thoughts are associated with this unforgiveness? How has it affected your well-being and relationships? What steps can you take to begin the process of forgiveness?

_____

_____

_____

_____

_____

_____

2. Consider a time when you experienced the power of forgiveness in your own life. How did forgiving someone impact your well-being and sense of freedom? Are there any similar situations where you can extend the same forgiveness to others?

_____

_____

_____

_____

_____

_____

3. Reflect on the complexities of forgiveness. Are there any misconceptions or misunderstandings about forgiveness that hinder your ability to extend it? How can you reframe your understanding to align with a more healing and transformative perspective?

_____

_____

_____

_____

_____

_____

4. Think about forgiveness as an ongoing journey. Are there any past hurts or offenses that you need to

revisit and extend forgiveness to again? What practices or techniques can you implement to maintain forgiveness and prevent the reseeding of resentment?

_____

_____

_____

_____

_____

_____

5. Reflect on the freedom and growth that forgiveness can bring. How has holding onto grudges or unforgiveness limited your personal growth and happiness? What possibilities open up when you choose to forgive and let go?

_____

_____

_____

_____

Self-Evaluation Questions

What are my strengths and weaknesses regarding the material covered in this Workbook?

_____

_____

_____

_____

What did I learn from this Workbook to apply to my life?

_____

_____

_____

_____

How can I improve my understanding of the material covered in this Workbook?

_____

_____

_____

_____

What are some specific goals that I can set for myself to improve my knowledge and skills in this area?

_____

_____

_____

_____

How can I share what I have learned from this Workbook with others?

_____

_____

_____

_____

Made in the USA
Las Vegas, NV
20 May 2024

90139192R00085